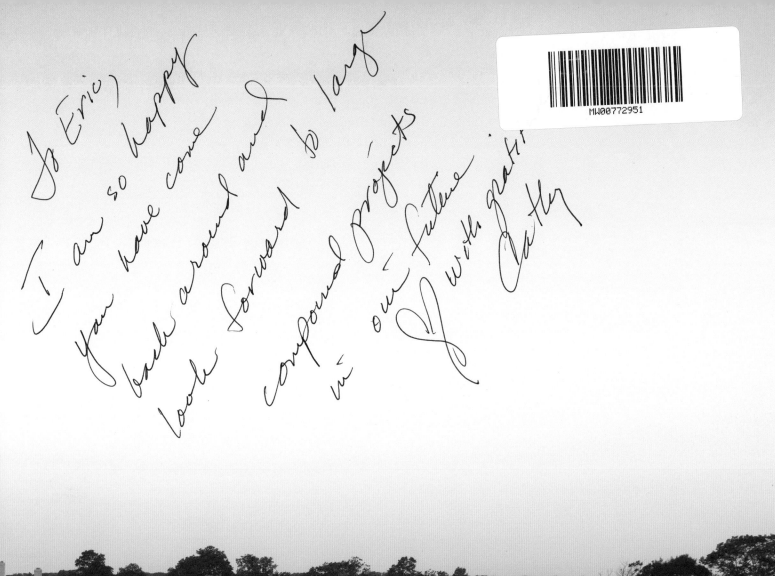

To Eric)
I am so happy
you have come
back around and
look forward to long
compound projects
in our future 💙 with gratit
Cathy

THE DESIGN OF A
COUNTRY ESTATE

THE DESIGN OF A
COUNTRY ESTATE

PURPLE CHERRY ARCHITECTS & INTERIORS

CATHY PURPLE CHERRY

PHOTOGRAPHS BY DURSTON SAYLOR

Gibbs Smith

CONTENTS

FOREWORD

Kevin Campion, Landscape Architect

They say that if you want to lift yourself up, you start by lifting up someone else. This is the embodiment of working with Cathy Cherry. I have had the pleasure of working closely with Cathy on dozens of projects over the past twenty years. In each instance, I have witnessed her skillful ability to build a talented team, inspire collaboration, and achieve refined outcomes. Her way of bringing homeowners, designers, and builders together with a shared purpose is remarkable. Her projects are spirited journeys towards a common goal of excellence.

A quick and acute thinker, Cathy has a keen ability to work through issues and respond in real time with creative solutions to challenging problems. She dissects issues on both large and small scales. She is capable of visualizing large, bold gestures in one moment and then focus on narrow, complex problems in the next. This skill allows her to keep information flowing, projects moving, and fees reasonable.

Cathy is a relentless, hardworking business owner who cares deeply about her team and her clients. She is disarming in her approach to client relations. She brings vivacity, sometimes crassness, and always laughter to her daily meetings. Clients become loyal to Cathy because of her brutal honesty, her interminable energy, and her unwavering commitment to the successful realization of each project.

Teamwork begins by building trust. The Purple Cherry Architecture staff chooses to bury egos below creative skillfulness and strong project management, and they support Cathy through a thoughtful process that engenders both confidence and trust. They shepherd project teams with a friendly and approachable manner, but also push hard to keep deadlines and budgets intact. This results in clients being satisfied with both the final product but also with the process.

Lastly, Cathy and her team are givers. They sustain an internal spirit that inherently puts others before themselves. This is exemplified time and time again as they go above and beyond to help others who are struggling. I have seen them show grace and compassion when clients have been sick or have lost a spouse. They show this same empathy towards coworkers and friends dealing with losses. It is simply who Cathy and her team are, and it resonates in everything they do. This is a blessing to those who have the pleasure to know Cathy and to work with the Purple Cherry Architects & Interiors team.

INTRODUCTION

In 1993, when I started my architectural practice in Annapolis, Maryland, it was one of two female-owned architecture firms in the city. My younger self did not imagine that someday I would have five office locations and a staff of nearly forty people or an in-house interior design division. I certainly knew I loved architecture and interior design and wanted to one day create beautiful homes. I never imagined that I would have such fantastic clients who would allow me to do what I truly love for a living and on such a large scale with multiple structures. It has truly been a life blessing.

I will say my younger self did know that I would someday own my own firm. People often ask me the origins of the firm's name: Why Purple Cherry Architects? I was born Catherine Purple and married a man by the name of Mike Cherry more than four decades ago. Given my plans to start my own firm one day, I made Purple my middle name and took on my husband's last name, and voilà—I became Cathy Purple Cherry, which also made for a very memorable company name.

From the beginning, my mind was clear about my approach to design and the business of architecture. I am first a faith-based person; honesty and transparency are incredibly important to me. I am very direct when it comes to process, time line, and costs. I work hard to protect my clients through the process, as does my talented team. I am not a "starchitect." I am never going to

say, "this is the only way," when, truthfully, there are many ways to accomplish something beautiful.

When I begin a project, I interview my clients about their lifestyle and living patterns and listen closely. This requires a very personal relationship. On occasion, design meetings call for more challenging conversations between my clients and their partners, so I keep a lighthearted yet serious demeanor and steer them towards solutions that can accommodate both their needs. Some clients tell me I would make a very good therapist! Asking the right questions makes for a more informed and successful result in designed living spaces. I have collaborative relationships with my clients because we all want the same outcome—a beautifully designed and constructed home that uniquely serves them and that they will love from day one and every day after.

As a sensitive and intuitive person, I am extremely attuned to people's physical and emotional health. One of my siblings was born with Down syndrome and one of my children is on the autism spectrum, so the well-being of everyone around me is always first and foremost in my practice. I am proud of these characteristics and the considerations I take throughout the design process, and I believe they bond me to my clients. This caring approach is instilled in each member of my firm, thus ensuring the same philosophy is carried forth in all our work.

While all my clients are involved in the design process, David Williams, the owner of Northwest Point Farm, was one of the most engaged I've ever worked with. His wife Kathryn joined occasionally for meetings, but David was the lead decision-maker, not only because he had been envisioning a compound like this before they met but also because he is versed in architectural concepts and knew what he wanted. And I was 1,000% happy with that. I didn't end up spinning my wheels or going down the wrong path.

David's dream about this property took root when he was young and owned a landscape maintenance company. He would mow lawns on large estates in Bucks County, Pennsylvania, with various outbuildings on them, like pump houses, barns, and greenhouses, and he became enamored with both the classical architectural style and rambling nature of the landscape. He personally drew the basic structure of the main house of Northwest Point Farm when he was in high school.

While David is an incredibly successful business professional, he has a huge respect for good design and enjoyed the whole journey of creating each structure from start to finish. His vision was a compound where thirty plus people could gather on Thanksgiving or other occasions, a truly welcoming family home and supporting buildings that had the same casual spirit.

From our first meeting, David would arrive at the office with stacks of tear sheets from publications, photocopies from architectural books, and even hand-drawn sketches that he had doodled while on his business travels. What David sought was an architect that deeply listened to him and respected his opinions. He knew I was never going to shut him down completely with an "absolutely not." Sometimes I would guide him towards a more feasible solution, and he learned to trust me as a professional; we developed a very considerate and respectful lasting relationship that allows us to rapidly bounce ideas off each other in our ongoing work.

As I thought about Northwest Point Farm, certain words took hold in my mind: traditional, classic, romantic, authentic, timeless, togetherness, and approachable elegance. The end result speaks to all of that and more. What you will discover in this book is how a family estate like this one unfolds from the lay of the land to the intricate architectural details. The nuances may not be evident at first sight but contribute to an eloquent and extraordinary experience.

This book reveals our thought processes and how we approached the goals of our client to deliver this envisioned utopian home. And because I am a straight shooter, you'll also find practical sidebars that cover topics that come into play in any commission, no matter the project scale. Every home design project is a carefully crafted journey from the big picture to the particulars, from the mathematical calculations to the emotional responses. I hope you find inspiration throughout these pages, whether your dream is a cozy cabin in the woods or an expansive country estate like Northwest Point Farm.

THE PROPERTY

This extraordinary 152-acre property in Centreville, Maryland, on the Eastern Shore along the Chester River is less than an hour's drive from Annapolis and only one-and-a-half hours from Washington, D.C. Its location makes it both easily accessible and highly desirable. The river horseshoes around this point of land in a wide, graceful bend creating an expansive engagement with the water, making this property a beautiful rarity.

In addition to the water's peninsula, another draw for our client to the property was its authenticity as a working farm. Most of the land was intentionally preserved for farming, sustained by a cluster of vernacular farm buildings that can be viewed along the entry drive. These farm structures that dot the bucolic landscape did not interfere with David's overall vision for the property. Instead, they provided an authentic expression of rural living on Maryland's Eastern Shore. Additionally, buffer areas between fields and shoreline were transitioned into hayfields, providing habitat diversity and a new collection of walking paths. A pond was dug to aid in irrigation and to offer fishing opportunities to guests. In general, all additions to the pastoral farm were intentional yet discreet and were sensitively stitched into the existing contextual landscape.

As stewards of the natural beauty that God has created, our firm strives to honor the unique and beautiful settings of all projects. We work to make sure anything we create lives up to the natural beauty of the property. When deciding where to site the main house on Northwest Point Farm, we took into consideration where the sun sets and rises, what you see across the river along the main house's view axis, and, of course, the extensive panoramic vistas. Many clients with water properties believe they need to be as close to the water as possible; typically, that is 100 feet from its edge. But when you have an expansive vista like this property offers, you have the same connection to the water whether you are 100 feet or 300 feet away. David visualized the main structure being on top of a knoll. To achieve this, we raised the property under the main house four feet, and in doing so, created a different perspective and a stepped strategy for the pool and pool house, which I'll discuss in further detail later in the book.

Many clients focus on wanting views from every angle and in every space of their homes. What they don't realize is that over time, the views simply become the backdrop to daily living. You don't want to sacrifice anything in the house's design for the sake of the views; you want it to be an engaging cohesive experience. That said, we are always committed to siting the house to take advantage of views whenever possible. Natural light is also an overarching priority in any house we design. We closely examine the

direction of the sun, how it moves over a property, and the way that affects the light in the interiors. Sunlight is so essential to our physical and mental well-being; we wanted to capture all that we could throughout this home.

What you will experience in the landscape itself is also a critical factor in planning phases. When beginning any project, but especially one of this scale, we always bring in a landscape architect to collaborate and help realize all the goals in the development of a property. Landscape design and the physical architecture go hand in hand to create a whole. You can't have the same experience if one is neglected; we plan ahead so both can be realized, often concurrently. For this special property, Kevin Campion of Campion Hruby Landscape Architects, who I have worked with many times

before, was the natural fit. He is gifted at capturing vistas and creating poignant connections to the land; he's also skilled at managing large rural properties in particular. He excels at creating layers and details within the landscape that engage the senses while fitting seamlessly within the whole.

The approach to the compound was a key element of the curated experience for Campion Hruby. While many Eastern Shore farms are approached via a long, tree-lined drive, it felt more natural to allow Northwest Point Farm

The property unfolds along a curving, bucolic road. It was originally a working farm, and some acreage is still devoted to agriculture. OVERLEAF: The approach to the compound includes an encounter with black sheep grazing in a center field. PAGES 16-17: To escape the elements, the sheep have a shed that resembles a charming cottage with a cupola and weather vane.

to unfold slowly and sequentially for family and guests to enjoy.

After initially entering the property at a small gatehouse, you only drive straight a short way before the axial disappears. You then enter a long, graceful curve and at once, your shoulders begin to relax as you take in the initial views of the farm. As you progress, you start to feel a sense of ease; you see the house, then the road dips down and it disappears, which creates some anticipation of what's ahead. After turning in the direction of the main house, you come upon a loop where you are immediately intrigued by a charming fieldstone structure topped with a cupola and a weather vane.

As you continue around the loop, your gaze turns to the black sheep grazing in a field, and you realize that whole area is devoted to the sheep with a fence that curves all the way around, and there's an aha moment—that small building is a sheep shed! And that sense of discovery as you traverse from the gatehouse to the sheep pasture is just the beginning. Approaching the main house, you enter a large, fenced courtyard that begins to organize the village of structures around you. You have arrived.

The migratory flight of Canadian geese across Maryland's Eastern Shore is a yearly ritual. OPPOSITE: Far removed from the house sits a quiet spot for fishing. Farm fields and meadow provide a layered backdrop. OVERLEAF: A stone wall and pump house accent the pond's edge and provide a healthy recharge of water.

THE COMPOUND

Imagine a place where multiple generations of family and dear friends can gather to share experiences that you have curated in every respect, a place that draws people together to find deeper connections and make meaningful memories that resonate long after any social media posts have faded. Whether it's family celebrations, holiday gatherings, pool parties, or simply relaxing and communing with each other in an idyllic setting, this is the romantic dream served up in a walkable family compound at Northwest Point Farm designed for generations to come.

Our task as the design team was to lean into that idealistic vision of large group gatherings and bring the client's dreams to fruition through thoughtful and thorough planning at all stages during the compound's realization. This planning was from the siting of the property down to the last interior details of each structure. When we started meeting with David to put the site plan together, we initially discussed the main house, guest cottage, and entertaining barn, but as discussions progressed, more structures came onboard and grander ideas for the property were fleshed out.

First though, we had to discuss the layout of the buildings and their relationships to each other. We focused on a "walkable estate," which over the course of my practice, I have found to

be a compelling concept. If structures are more closely related to each other, you will use all of them. If you make them too far apart, you will use them less frequently—inconvenience being the driving factor. Who wants to drive a Gator or golf cart after an elegant dinner party to reach the guest quarters?

Regardless of the size of a property, in order to experience each building comfortably within a daily routine, the connections between buildings need to be intuitive. In our design, we created symmetrical links among the structures and then connected that symmetry with very linear and logical walking paths. We honored the power of center axes among the buildings and paths. This organized connectivity creates a calming presence on the property. And from a purely aesthetic view, a walkable estate where the buildings are in conversation with each other evokes graceful symmetry and harmony within the larger landscape.

Through experience, I have found that an average of 100 feet between buildings and about 400 feet from one far side of the layout to the other is ideal. Our firm uses an advanced modeling software that allows us to load in potential structures and see everything in 3D to determine how to place each structure within the property. We start tweaking from there. Of course, we ultimately stake the modeling to the

building footprints on the site itself to determine if our parameters and instincts are correct.

When we started this project in 2015, Purple Cherry Architects had approximately fifteen employees, so it simply was not feasible to build everything at the same time and do it right. We were very strategic about which buildings would be built first. Obviously, most clients are anxious to move into the main house, but more practical concerns often take precedence. We needed a place to store all the construction materials away from the elements and a place for the builder to run operations. We started with the carriage house and garage to serve those purposes.

Next, construction on the guest cottage began. This allowed our clients to start enjoying the property while the main house was completed, which took three years. In a project of this scope, multiple things are happening at the same time.

Construction doesn't progress in a linear fashion; most of the construction efforts run parallel or overlap with each other.

For example, while the main house was going up, so was the entertaining barn. We had to keep everything moving along to have any prayer of the compound being completed within the five-year time line that started with our first introduction to David. In building, if you make changes to one structure, it can affect an adjacent one. A compound involves a series of moving parts, and when working on a project of this scale, you must be hyper-focused on details while still looking at the big picture.

An aerial view of the compound reveals how the various buildings relate to each other in the landscape to create a walkable experience.

If I've learned anything about working on compounds, it is that a willingness to pivot and make changes even after the framing goes up is essential. A project like this could not be completed in a timely fashion without some on-the-spot decision-making and an incredibly dedicated team of design and construction professionals who are on the same page and willing to put their egos aside throughout the process.

We were also extraordinarily fortunate to have a fantastic client who had a very specific vision for each structure and for the estate as a whole, yet also trusted the project team to implement what we thought was best. This is the perfect formula for a beautiful and functional design. David trusted us on everything from broad vision to microscopic trim and tile details, lighting and color effects, furniture and accessory selections, and final furniture placement for move in. The joy of the journey was the ongoing opportunities continuously given to the design team by this incredible client to focus on all kinds of creative possibilities.

RIGHT: The river horseshoes around a point of land, allowing for an expansive engagement with the water throughout the compound. OVERLEAF: The connections between the structures are very organized and intuitive and a breeze to navigate. There is an average of 100 feet between buildings and 400 feet from one far side to the other.

THE MAIN HOUSE

No matter how long you practice architecture, it's still a humbling experience when someone trusts you to design a home where their day in and day out life will unfold. It's much more than a house plan; you hope to fulfill their expectations of how they envision this new chapter in their lives. During the process, we think about all those "moments" that play out in each room, from preparing for the day to cooking a family meal. There's responsibility, but also great joy in taking on this kind of design. And whether the house is 500 square feet or several thousand, we take the same approach and throw ourselves into emotionally supporting our clients with our designs.

David loves traditional design, particularly the architecture of Colonial Williamsburg, so all the buildings on this property dial into the notion of "the new/old house." This is architecture that offers an emotional thread to the past but has all the creature comforts of a modern lifestyle. It focuses on authentic historic design principles using quality building materials that will stand up to time as a new home starts to age. Every structure in this compound was designed to resonate for generations to come. When deciding how the various new/old buildings should relate to each other visually, we focused on cohesion in the materials and repeating design motifs in the architecture.

If you have buildings dotted all throughout a large property, you can take more liberties with the styles represented, but in a walkable compound, given the close connections, you want everything to present beautifully as a whole. Depending on each building and its use, we employed eyebrow dormers, sunlit cupolas, handmade Cushwa oversized brick, custom shutters, native fieldstone, and white cedar shake zinc-coated copper roofs. They speak to each other in the same language and color tones, but their dialect varies through differing roof forms and material applications. We wanted to avoid any feeling of too much sameness, yet we desired a cohesive community.

EXTERIOR

On the outside of the main house, our client wanted a classic, stately Georgian-style country home, which is reflected in both the design and the materials. A lot of the water-view houses in the area are red cedar and copper so they get that brown, burnished look over time. This house is completely different—it's intended to be grayish and white, so we used white cedar shingles for the roofs. If the roof on this house had been slate, it would have created an entirely different emotional experience; the cedar takes down the formality, is more in sync with the setting, and evokes a welcoming presence as you approach.

PAGES 28–29: A modestly scaled front entrance brings down the formality of the facade and imparts a welcoming presence. OVERLEAF: The stately Georgian-style exterior speaks to the power of symmetry. PAGES 32–33: Zinc-coated copper roofs provide continuity among many of the buildings and the connecting covered walkways. PAGE 34–35: Each end of the main house exterior has a columned, L-shaped porch that connects to the rear of the house. PAGES 36–37: The back of the main house continues the study in symmetry and includes enclosed screened-in porches on either end that provide for more versatility in use.

Roofing Materials

A roof makes a very powerful statement because of its scale on the exterior of a home. Its color and amount of vertical exposure in a design are very important decisions, which clients do not always realize. Sometimes the reason they fell in love with or had a meaningful connection with a particular style of house is because of the roofing materials. Perhaps cedar or slate are not in the budget, and when they see their roof design rendered in asphalt, their attraction wanes. The process educates them about the distinction a roof can make. Some clients ultimately decide to put their dollars towards a more beautiful yet costly roof material and give up other things in the design scheme to achieve the desired look.

Manufactured Wood-Look Option

If you can believe it, all the "wooden" siding and trim on most structures is a manufactured, mostly recycled product that's more expensive but behaves like wood in the best ways but not in the worst ways. It can be painted where brushstrokes are evident for a naturalistic look, but it's impervious to the elements and does not rot. A few clients are material purists and are willing to replace wooden window sills, trim, and decking every seven to fifteen years as needed, but more and more of my clients want their homes to require less maintenance, especially in sizable new builds.

The design with a central hallway allows views from the front door through to the water beyond. OPPOSITE: The graceful entry hallway sets the tone for the interiors with compelling millwork, French doors, and transom windows. A series of large, antique brass lanterns provide a moody glow in the evening.

INTERIOR

The main home's façade offers a study in the beauty of symmetry. It presents a uniform and elegant attitude with repeating elements such as Doric columns, dormers, and shed roofs, among others. If you split the house in two, the sides would be almost identical. You initially step onto an inviting front porch under a classic columned portico. Then you enter through the mahogany front door framed by sidelights and a transom window into a large central hallway or core, which extends to the rear of the house. The natural splendor of the property is front and center when stepping over the threshold. And when you stand in the long entry hall, you can see all the way to the end of both sides of the house as well as up to the second floor through a balcony. It is truly a moment of delightful engagement and anticipation.

The formal symmetry of the home's exterior and layout is balanced by its personal, welcoming interiors. There is nothing fussy or overwrought

in the design; it's simply comfortable and supports the interior architecture in the best way. There are references to the countryside and the coast throughout this home that give it a farmhouse spirit in harmony with the setting. One thing immediately apparent in the interiors is the extensive millwork. It is a unifying element that gives this large home a comfortable and approachable living scale.

The first floor is divided into zones, so to speak. On the left of the house sit the hardworking and multipurpose areas: the hunt room, kitchen, and back kitchen. In the middle are the living spaces: two mirror-sized living rooms on either side of the central hall, the dining room, and library. The right side contains the entertaining/party spaces: billiard room, a built-in bar area, and a cozy small living room. David's office is there as well to provide some separation from the busier rooms in the house.

A round mahogany table sits in the entry hallway that leads to the living and family rooms, introduced by a pair of chests topped with bronze sculptures and art specifically chosen by our client. OPPOSITE: The stairway features classic and refined architectural details, while the eyebrow window floods the upper level with abundant light.

LIVING SPACES

Our interior design team worked to achieve balance in the overall feel of the home; it's not too casual or too stiff. The palette and fabrics in this home firmly sit in the neutral camp with doses of blue in many spaces. You will not see any wild or busy patterns in play such as big florals. Likewise, the furniture reads more streamlined, with no ornately carved chairs or lacquered cabinets.

The millwork throughout this house is exceptional and accomplishes many purposes. On the first floor, where the main living spaces are open to each other, millwork defines each space and imparts a beautiful sense of classic gravitas. In the two living rooms, each with its own fireplace, we designed a wall of French doors with transoms, so you're always in conversation with the outside and water views. The two spaces share a common palette and decorating style, although one reads as more casual and has the television while the other one leans more formal with a writing desk.

When an expanse of green lawn and blue water surrounds you at almost every turn, you don't want the interiors to compete with that. The décor is more like a supporting player paying homage to the natural landscape—which is why someone purchases a property like this in first place. We introduced a lot of textures and varying materials to add interest and keep the eye moving around the

The right-side living room is filled with sink-into upholstery to take in the views or enjoy a crackling fire in the evenings. Blue hues feel in harmony with the water, which is in constant conversation with the interiors.

spaces. Brick, beadboard, tile, metal finishes, sisal, Douglas fir, brass, and leather all play a part.

Another layer of texture comes from the decorative touches. I always say that a house does not feel like a home until all the "stuff" starts to layer in, dispersing any impression of coldness or severity. Artwork is a paramount consideration in completing the interiors and our clients wholeheartedly agreed. David and Kathryn started collecting art once the property was purchased in 2013. They bought what they loved as they travelled, knowing it was destined for the farm. I love that the art is distributed throughout the main house with abundance, even in unexpected places. I also love the array of colors and subjects introduced by the art.

We wanted to ensure that the art collection would be shown to its best advantage. Some decisions regarding millwork and lighting were made around certain pieces of art once their placement was decided. David's family has been in the art business for generations, and he has developed a great appreciation for how best to display art and draw the eye towards it. And believe it or not, he hung every last piece himself.

This house is large enough that it called for a formal dining room for our client's family to have special meals together for holidays and other celebratory occasions (see pages 58–59). The debate among our team was whether the table should be formal or more casual; the casual camp won. The architecture may be classic and buttoned up, but the furnishings and décor read as more informal, and we didn't want this room to feel like a disconnect from the whole.

A large, graceful archway connects the dining room to the central hall, while another identical arch welcomes you into the library opposite. The library is one of my favorite rooms in the house. It is truly a special space. Our client gave us the go-ahead to develop a double-layer millwork room, or a room inside of a room, meaning that there's an inner plane that does one thing and then an outer plane that does another thing. We wanted to create special moments throughout this room, starting with two leather-topped built-in benches that flank the fireplace, and then we added ample bookcases around the perimeter.

Detailed millwork used throughout the main floor helps to both define and link the spaces. OPPOSITE: One living area shows off brass accents in the chandelier, sconces, and desk lamps. OVERLEAF: French doors on the back of the living spaces allow for fresh air and create a great flow between the interiors and the entertaining spaces beyond.

PAGES 48–49: The deep. columned back porch has separate areas for dining and lounging in comfortable style. PRECEDING OVERLEAF: Orderly brick pathways make it easy to traverse from the rear porch to the pool and pool house. ABOVE: The custom wooden dining table can handle a crowd with seating for up to twelve guests, and its weathered surface can stand up to wear and weather. OPPOSITE: A screened-in porch on the rear of the house and off the kitchen provides an additional option for dining. OVERLEAF: A book lover's dream of a library has book cases around the room and generous chairs for curling up with a bestseller.

Two unique built-in benches provide the perfect spots for fireside reading. OPPOSITE: The powder bath vanity nestles inside an elegant arched niche. OVERLEAF: Off the center hall sits the inviting dining room with warm wooden furnishings and comfortable, fully upholstered leather chairs.

KITCHEN

Most people desire a kitchen that opens to the family room, but this client wanted a more compartmentalized design to realize that classic center core I referenced earlier. In a larger home, you can create smaller casual seating areas within the kitchen environment that function like a mini family room, which is what we did here.

When designing kitchens, I focus on a layout that will keep people out of the prep and working area, so the person preparing the food can address the tasks at hand without interruption. Any other needs or functions for the room are placed outside that space. This particular kitchen is a house unto itself. On one end sits the heavy work area with a large island that includes a prep sink. Beyond that is another island that, while not for seating, helps to divide the room. Custom made with a zinc top and painted a coastal blue, it acts like a piece of furniture and provides a color connection to the hunt room. This island has storage for additional utensils and dishware, while the drawers hold table linens and the like.

Beyond that is another dividing element, a custom-designed breakfast table with an iron base and wood top. At the end of the kitchen is a seating area with chairs flanking a fireplace and French doors on either side that lead to a screened-in dining porch.

Given the space's overall size, we had room to set up distinct serving areas against the perimeter—a coffee bar and a wine/spirits bar. A combination pot rack and lighting fixture with its

gleaming copper pans beautifully encapsulates the heartbeat of the kitchen.

We also included a pass-through serving station with glass-front cabinetry that lets in light and frames a view of the stairway beyond with its reclaimed Chicago brick wall. Chicago

brick is used in many parts of the house; its roughness and imperfections bring instant character and texture to a space. Any reclaimed materials or vintage pieces are always welcome in new construction to impart a sense of age and authenticity.

A beadboard ceiling and a blue-painted custom storage island bring nautical touches to the spacious multiuse kitchen. OVERLEAF: A large-scale picture window over the sink embraces the pastoral setting, while glass-front cabinetry adds an informal cottage accent.

OPPOSITE Brick appears in both the exterior and interior, adding more rustic moments in the design, such as this stairway wall right off the kitchen. ABOVE: A handsome, built-in storage and gun display cabinet in a gray-blue tone with wood paneling features a place to highlight one of the many outstanding art pieces in the home. OVERLEAF: A clever cabinet design in the kitchen features glass-front and -back display cabinets that let more light into the space.

Balancing Lifestyle
with Design

When I begin working with clients, I
like to discuss their trigger points and
pet peeves. I believe in having honest
and sometimes challenging conversations
with my clients from the start. We are all
wired differently and have varying degrees
of tolerance for certain conditions. One
partner may complain about something
that the other one simply does not care
about. I am also a firm believer in the idea
that "you can't always teach an old dog new
tricks." I strive to find an acceptable middle
ground or compromise that accommodates
each partner's needs and provides physical
and mental comfort.

For example, from a design perspective,
I like to address my clients' storage
style before determining the layout and
materials for the main and back kitchens.
If a client is more organized and inclined
to put everything back in its place, I love
incorporating glass-front cabinets or
open shelves where kitchen items can be
displayed and styled for all to see. For those
who lean towards a more erratic system,
I plan for materials and architectural
decisions that aid in concealment, like
adding a pocket door that leads to the
living spaces, so the kitchen can be closed
off from view. What we all want at the end
of the day is to experience life in our homes
in a happy and meaningful way, and that's
what our firm passionately strives to create
in our designs.

BACK KITCHEN

A back kitchen adjoins the main kitchen and includes a glass-front refrigerator (additional appliances are ready for when there's a crowd) and a small, rustic butcher block island. People can help themselves to snacks and drinks in here without bothering the cook. Even if space is tighter, I always place the trash and refrigerator on the outside of the cooking space to help with circulation. We chose the same white subway tile used in the hunt room for the walls, which provides some continuity, but instead of weathered red brick floors, we added striking gray brick laid in a herringbone pattern and some open shelving. We placed a large, framed chalkboard for to-do lists and doodling, which lets you know this is a casual space. This pass-through room connects to the formal dining room and can be closed off by a pocket door.

OPPOSITE TOP: The back kitchen leads to the dining room and provides ample storage and options for cleanup and food prep. OPPOSITE BELOW: A framed chalkboard offers both practical uses like grocery lists and more whimsical ones such as doodling or secret messages.

Pros and Cons of a Back Kitchen

I am often asked about the fairly recent popularity of the back kitchen, and I have a strong opinion about it—I love it! Going back a few decades, when TV shows started sharing kitchens with a highly organized look—labeled containers and designated places for everything— people started thinking that was normal. Combined with the emergence of retailers dedicated to organization and, of course, social media, younger generations don't grasp that life is messy.

Also, the women of my generation are tired of family members dumping stuff everywhere in the kitchen, and if they are building a retirement or second home and anticipating visits from grandchildren and extended family, the prospect of a back kitchen is appealing.

The only drawback to a back kitchen is when it is so much like a main kitchen that it takes the parents away from communal family time, like kids doing homework at the kitchen island or simply talking about their day. I've seen that happen when one of the parents wants to present a pristine kitchen to potential guests. The way to avoid this is to omit a stove and oven from the back kitchen. This forces all cooking into the main kitchen. Remember, we don't live in a photo shoot; life is wonderfully imperfect. Learning this early can be helpful to maintaining long-term relationships.

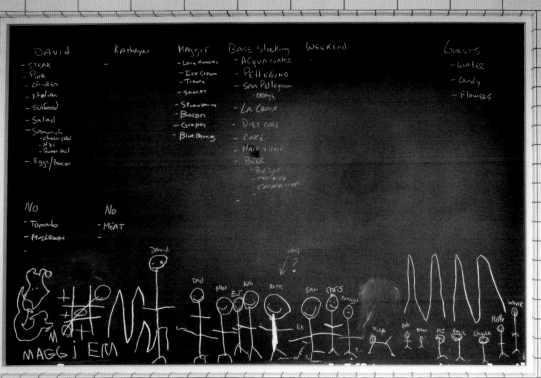

Views and the play of natural light throughout the house featured heavily in all design decisions, including this sunroom space off the kitchen, which embraces the shore and sunny days with stylish ease.

HUNT ROOM

We call this space a "hunt room" because it's much more than a typical mudroom, and its origins are rooted in tradition. Historically, this is where people entered after completing a hunt before stepping into any other room in the house. This space offers open storage, including options for hanging and placing gear, soiled clothing, and boots. It also has a long center table in the middle for dropping groceries, mail, packages, and the like. Most mudrooms are a pass-through space with closed storage cabinetry meant to disguise the chaos and are quite modest in scale.

Given the size of the home, we had an opportunity to create an authentic-style hunt room accessed through a breezeway from the garage. This is the everyday entrance for family and friends. Two entry Dutch doors in this room are painted blue,

as is the front door of the guest cottage, as a nod to the water beyond. Dutch doors have a farmhouse history dating from the 17th-century. They are divided, so that the top can be opened while the lower portion is closed. The original purpose was to keep farm animals out while allowing a breeze inside, but today, they add a layer of charm and authenticity to a country home.

In this space are the expected lockers to hold coats, shoes, and backpacks, but the hunt room also includes a powder bath with fun dog print wallpaper and a pantry closet with an old-fashioned golden metal mesh inset in the door. On the room's opposite side, a custom potting shed/floral arranging unit has open shelving above, a sink for easy cleanup, and firewood storage below. We painted the unit blue, which gives it a distinct identity in the space. The reclaimed brick floors provide warmth and old-world character and can take a beating. A heavily weathered table placed in the center is perfect for crafts and other projects—bring on the glitter and markers, this surface will only become more lovingly patinaed over time! We used beadboard in this room and V-groove paneling, with more beadboard in many parts of the home, on ceilings and walls, which speaks to the coast with their nautical leanings and brings a welcome casualness.

Vintage wire baskets add to the charm of the hunt room. OPPOSITE: There is plenty of open storage and locker space. A long, weathered table and rustic stools are convenient for multiple uses. OVERLEAF: The hunt room takes cues from both kitchens with its beadboard ceiling and white subway tiles, but the brick floor sets it apart.

SLEEPING SPACES

Two symmetrical staircases at either end of the house lead from the main floor to the lower level and to the second floor. The third-floor staircase is centered above the front door creating a powerful impact upon entering the house. When arriving on the landing of the second floors by both end staircases, you see the triple chandeliers that we had custom made, which light the two stairwells and create drama. This also eliminated the need for multiple sconces along the brick walls. We included porthole windows to brighten the stairway with natural light. It's always a win if we find practical solutions that are also a pleasure to experience.

The second floor is divided into two wings: the primary suite on one side and the guest rooms on the other. In the primary suite, pocket doors lead to an entry vestibule; the bedroom sits on the right, water side, and the closets and bathroom are on the left, field side. The suite can be totally shut off from the rest of the floor for privacy and noise reduction when guests are afoot. The bedroom here has glorious long views of the water, which we wanted to capture and take full advantage of in the design. To allow the bed to face the water, we created an interior wall unit with built-in bedside tables and bookcases and an arched interior transom window at the top which lets in more natural light to the dressing room area in the suite. The headboard sits against it and looks out on the water while French doors flanking the fireplace lead out to a balcony.

A primary bedroom suite should speak to unwinding and romance, and honestly both are more likely to occur when the space functions well day in and day out. I believe in compartmentalizing the bedroom suite when possible. Couples are often not wired the same, and the habits of both people using the space should be taken into account for maximum comfort in both the layout and in such details as lighting and access to outlets. I typically wake up early while my husband of forty plus years is still sleeping, so I am laser-focused on accommodating these differences in the planning stages.

The goal is to have the busyness of the suite take place outside of the bedroom. Here there is a separate dressing room with custom built-ins and a center island chest of drawers. Given the size of the suite, we included a windowed laundry room, which is a welcome convenience. The adjoining bathroom has a soaking tub tucked into an arched alcove with a complementary large, arched window that looks over the property and a big walk-in shower. Kathryn wanted a seated mirrored vanity, so the layout needed to accommodate that as well.

One thing people don't always realize is that the outside architecture often informs what you

Staircases on either end of the home feature custom triple chandeliers to light the way and to add a unique decorative element. OVERLEAF: Between the two bedroom wings, we placed a beadboard arched reading niche complete with bookcases, sconces, and art.

can do inside. This bathroom is a prime example of that principle. It's an unusually shaped room with different ceiling heights, low walls in places, and dormers with arched gables. The challenge in this space was how to create common sense out of the eccentric things happening and have it function as desired. This is one of my greatest joys and where the math happens. I love making sense out of abstract or odd-shaped spaces. In our practice at Purple Cherry Architects & Interiors, we do not let obstacles get in the way of good design decisions.

The long connecting hall between the two wings houses a mini library with curved built-in seating and bookshelves tucked in on either side, all behind a graceful arch that sets off the space and makes it more of a destination. It's a perfect place to perch while waiting for a partner or to escape when you need a little alone time. This space leads to the guest wing and a series of bedrooms: two with a view of the water and two with a view of the grazing sheep. Each bedroom is decorated differently and has an en suite bathroom. At the end of the hall opposite the primary suite, Douglas fir windows look down on the bar below from the large, multipurpose primary guest suite.

The bedroom in the primary guest suite claims the most significant view and connects to an outdoor balcony with French doors on either side of the fireplace, just like the primary bedroom. In this room, we used interior windows to allow natural light from the outer core to the inner core and also to transfer the view from the inner core to the water view space beyond.

Outside of the bed area are the functional areas, including a built-in serving alcove with a sink, mini refrigerator, and open shelving above. To the side of that is a curved banquette with a table, elevated to allow anyone sitting there—perhaps working on a laptop—to experience a full view of the water through the bedroom's interior windows. We work on many view properties and interior windows work so well in those settings; it's become a signature of the firm.

Stunning Calacatta marble encases the primary guest bathroom with built-in storage and mirrored upper cabinets that give it the feel of a dressing room. In between the two ceiling-height mirrored cabinets sits a low storage unit, topped by a row of steel bars—this is where you place your luggage.

When space allows, we like the guest quarters to be self-contained so everyone can take care of their needs without having to go elsewhere. We included a hall laundry room that all guests can access. Over the washer/dryer is a soapstone folding counter with hanging space above. Another counter placed in front of the window features a sink, with laundry baskets below. Inside the laundry room, is what I call the "self-serve open closet." It's one of my favorite components in this house. You will find the towels here, but also a host of organized items from shampoo to razors,

The bed in the primary suite sits against an interior wall unit to take advantage of the views. A vintage Louis Vuitton trunk at the foot of the bed doubles as a table. OVERLEAF: The pale blue walls in the primary bedroom speak to the setting beyond, enjoyed from anywhere in the room or on the private balcony.

so if you forget something, you are beautifully taken care of. We purposely did not include a door on this closet, so someone visiting for the first time can see into this space and know what's available for self-serve.

The third floor of the main house is dedicated to sleeping quarters for kids with four additional bedrooms and baths for when there's a big house party. In the mix, you find identical girls' and boys' bunk rooms, distinguished by their palettes. The girls' is turquoise and the boys' is navy; each room sleeps six. Bunk rooms for me are all about a "sitting around a campfire" spirit with conversations, ghost stories, and gossip. In some bunk rooms, the beds lay against solid walls and there's no connection. This design, configured in a U-shape, allows visual sight lines between everyone's heads, so they can see each other to chatter away late into the night. Between the bunk rooms and connected to the third-floor landing is a TV viewing space that contains a king-size custom window seat with a water view under an eight-foot-long eyebrow window. It's a cozy space to snuggle up in and it doubles as an additional sleeping area for big spend-the-night parties.

OPPOSITE: The spa-like primary bathroom's marble floor has a basket weave mosaic tile inset that runs along the center of the space, creating a beautiful punctuation mark. Over the vanity, we designed custom mirrors framed in white trim and attached sconces directly on the surface.

OPPOSITE: An arched window alcove provides lovely views from the soaking tub. ABOVE LEFT: A marble-topped island with multiple drawers keeps the primary suite closet clutter free. ABOVE RIGHT: The closet has built-in storage, some with mirrored, trimmed cabinet fronts and set against a blue floral wallpaper.

Details Matter

While I consider myself open-minded when it comes to design, there are a handful of things that drive me a bit crazy, such as adding a faucet directly into the drywall without a backsplash. I don't care what type of fixture it is; I know how people live and I know what your hands do! Other pet peeves include any details that create a distraction or a distortion of views. That could be anything from having a door crash into another door, being able to view a toilet from a living space, or even simply poor joinery. Details matter greatly, and anything that disrupts the overall design harmony sticks out and is visually unpleasant.

OPPOSITE: A hallway leads from the primary suite to the other end of the second floor, culminating in a multipurpose guest quarters that overlook the first-floor vaulted bar room.

For those needing a place to work, we included a desk right outside the bedroom and designed an elevated, curved banquette with a pedestal that allows for views while on task or enjoying an end-of-day cocktail. OPPOSITE: In view properties like this one, we often design an interior windowed wall so the bed can face the water while light bounces into the interior spaces beyond. OVERLEAF: Neutral tones for the walls and furnishings make for a warm and inviting atmosphere that will appeal to any guest, especially when a fireplace and private balcony are part of the experience.

One of guest bathrooms features a chevron mosaic marble tile wall, shiny penny tile floors, and a decidedly chic Lucite and polished nickel vanity. OPPOSITE: The largest guest bathroom exudes luxury with Calacatta marble floors and wainscotting, a soaking tub, and a built-in luggage rack with storage underneath. OVERLEAF: Each well-appointed guest room has sumptuous bedding, a mix of antiques and new upholstery, and a distinct style from the others.

OPPOSITE: The third floor is accessed by the elegant center stairway on view when stepping into the home. ABOVE: The third floor contains additional sleeping options for when there's a crowd. We included a lounge-television area with a built-in daybed. It is tucked under the eaves and in front of the eyebrow window, making it a favorite destination for young guests especially.

There are two bunk rooms on the third floor—one for girls and one for boys. The custom beds are set against beadboard walls and outfitted with individual sconces that impart cottage charm.

ENTERTAINING AND WORKING SPACES

The fun and games begin on the right side of the house. It's also where David's office is located, which may seem counterintuitive, but it makes good sense. This less frequently used area of the house provides our client privacy to accomplish his daily tasks.

While most of the home has white walls, this office is a departure with its moodier palette of dark slate blue that we wrapped around the entire room and softened with warm tones in the brown leather armchairs, flooring, and brass lighting.

To keep the room from feeling closed in, we included French doors that lead to the billiards area. A freestanding table versus a traditional desk and a neutral rug impart airiness. A porthole window to the bar beyond adds a little whimsy, and a hidden closet behind a bookcase panel feels like something out of a who-done-it mystery. Disguised doors often lead to another room, hide

such office support items as printers, or conceal a home safe.

You see the power of millwork in the billiards room as well. A curved Douglas fir beadboard ceiling over the pool table feels reminiscent of a ship's hull and sets this area apart. Specially designed ledges along the perimeter, topped with a slate slab inset, provide a place to set down cocktails in between play.

The waterfront side in this part of the home features a small den, which we call the "winter room." For us, a monochromatic dark color creates coziness, and this deep blue helps to bring down the ceiling height. There's a cocooning attitude that makes you want to snuggle up when the temperatures drop. And just like the kitchen, this space connects to an identical screened-in porch used for sitting outside around a wood-burning fireplace during cooler months.

OPPOSITE: A den off the right side of the house has deep-colored millwork and built-in book cases that create an inviting coziness and an ideal canvas for showcasing a series of sailing photographs. OVERLEAF: David's handsome office features deep blue nickel gap paneling and cabinetry and a porthole window that convey a nautical spirit. PAGES 106–07: The billiards space has all the bells and whistles for game play under a distinctive, curved, wood-paneled ceiling.

LEFT: With the doors open, the billiard room looks all the way to the opposite end of the house. OPPOSITE: The double-height ceiling in the bar called for some layered lighting solutions—two large, open iron lanterns, three downlight sconces, and four pendants over the bar itself.

BAR ROOM

At the very end of this side of the house sits the stepped down, built-in bar room. It's quite a spectacular space with a Chicago brick backdrop and a tall, vaulted ceiling that definitely adds a wow moment. Horizontal V-groove wood panels, used for the bar's base and on the walls, convey a playful, nautical vibe. A dartboard hides behind an interior shutter for when the mood strikes, and it's fun to show the reveal.

The double-story volume here was created for drama but also to integrate the bar into the primary guest suite on the second floor. Windows in that suite look down into the bar and are also framed in Douglas fir to provide some continuity between the two floors. A jib door offers another surprise in the bar. It opens to reveal a narrow stairway that leads to the lower level. If you run out of Pinot Noir upstairs, you can descend to the wine vault without having to go back through the house. As well as a conversational touch point, it also conjures up that feeling of going to a hidden speakeasy of yesteryear.

The bar features some clever design ideas such as bracketed ledges to hold drinks and a dartboard on an operable shutter that can be hidden away when not in use. RIGHT: A brick wall and floor and Douglas fir framing give the bar a distinctive and more rustic organic look. The windows at the top of the wall allow for views from the upstairs guest suite.

ENTERTAINING LOWER LEVEL

An entertaining basement like this one provides a rare opportunity to create a mood and atmosphere without thinking about how the sunlight will play out in the space. It's a welcome chance to come up with some creative ideas, which our client took to heart. David wanted a temperature-controlled wine vault and adjoining dining area with supporting spaces. I remember when he came in with a torn-out black-and-white newspaper article about how these types of vaulted brick caves are crafted in Mexico. He showed it to me and said, "Can we do that?" and I said, "That would be fantastic." It's very rare to have that kind of client and it's so exciting for me.

The mason and his team cut every groin brick on a miter and every piece was scored to conform to the design of the groin vaults in the ceiling. The room is a remarkable feat of masonry which took about eight months to complete. You really appreciate the hand of the craftsman in a project like this; to see it so immaculately realized can make you feel both elated and humbled.

When clients express concerns about the expense of any trade professionals, I take the time to educate them about the process and the costs. Without refined craftsmanship, the home they envisioned will not be realized; it simply will not look and feel the same. I help them understand that these skilled professionals and the associated

expenses are vital to the success of any project.

In addition to the Chicago brick masonry, another architectural trope repeats from the upper floors. Symmetry makes a continuing refrain throughout the compound, and this space is no exception. Two identical arches, one for entering from the upstairs bar and one for accessing the wine room, create harmony within the whole. Symmetry evokes a calmness that you sense but can't always put your finger on. Its roots date back to the classical architecture of ancient Greece and Rome—and it's a key reason that we are still drawn to enduring principles of design.

In the basement dining space, the furniture arrangement shows the value of versatility; two tables can be pulled together for larger events if needed, and we included a cozy built-in dining banquette for more intimate gatherings. A large, impressive interior porthole window brings a nautical nod and provides a striking punctuation mark against all that brick. It also draws your gaze into the wine room itself and pulls the eye up to appreciate the workmanship. The temperature-controlled cellar sits behind this windowed wall; it's a dark monochromatic room with ample built-in beverage storage and a simple table in the center.

Behind French doors are two other rooms that support the wine dining area when

entertaining: a post-tasting cleanup station that also stores the glassware and a catering kitchen with a wood-fired pizza oven for parties. The oven had to be crane-lowered into the basement before the floor above was even framed up. A pizza oven like this is a big masonry animal—it's basically a large, prebuilt fireplace with a chimney. Beyond, you will find a movie room with tiered seating and a candy cart in the corner, an exercise room, yoga studio, playroom, pantry space, dog-washing room, and all the impressive mechanics required to run this house, hidden behind closed doors.

What you won't find here are any sleeping spaces; there are many options for guests on the second and third floors or in the guesthouse, which keeps the intent of the lower level intact as a destination for entertaining and other activities.

The lower-level wine room showcases the skill of the artisan, who laid each brick by hand. OVERLEAF: It was important that the tasting room feel magical, so we created a glow with strategic lighting, and of course, candlelight helps set the mood.

Using glass-front cabinets in the tasting prep space, makes it easy to choose the appropriate wine glasses. Blue subway tile brings in some color and a little fun to this practical area.

Adapting to the Times

A basement is still a good idea if you want to have multiple places to entertain, exercise, and watch movies, but in most of our new builds, clients are foregoing a fully finished basement. Instead, we are doing deep crawl spaces for storage with lower ceiling heights. Not only are basements expensive, especially given the cost of concrete nowadays, but they simply aren't used the same way as in prior decades. Before technology, parents needed a place for the kids to play on rainy or cold days. Now children have computers and smart phones, so instead of heading to the basement, they are heading upstairs to their bedrooms to hang out with friends.

Also, dedicated destination wine vaults are not a priority for most of my clients, unless they are true wine collectors. Instead, we often put a small, glass-front wine closet on the first floor right off the family room with space to keep bottles at the ready. This solution is both functional and beautiful to look at.

A fully stocked catering-style kitchen with open stainless-steel shelving includes a movable work table on casters and a brick pizza oven for creating family favorites.

The intricate brickwork around the groin vaults in the ceiling is simply stunning. OPPOSITE: An arched hallway leads from the tasting room to the prep and kitchen spaces. We included a large-scale porthole window that sets off the wine storage room and creates a nautical focal point.

THE GUEST COTTAGE

This quaint cottage sits to the right of the main house and directly across from the entertaining barn. Guests enter from the central green quad or through the screened-in porch on the back of the house. The cottage is symmetrical and is built from similar materials to the other structures on the property, but it is more coastal in feel with nautical and industrial accents. We specified wall shingles on the upper gables to distinguish the guesthouse from the other buildings and to give it a more casual attitude.

The front entrance is enchanting from the first encounter. It's sited behind white picket fencing with fieldstone end posts, and pavers lead to a columned brick porch under a zinc-coated copper overhang. There sit two long custom benches in a cheerful Nantucket blue; this color is also used on the multipaned front door and for louvered shutters centered under the peak of the dormers. This is the same blue used on the main house hunt room exterior Dutch doors.

The porch's wraparound design was crafted specifically to take advantage of four viewing areas: the front porch looks out onto the green and the other structures; the right end gazes at a playful dancing sheep sculpture through an allée of trees; the left end looks onto the bocce court and boathouse folly; and the rear draws the eye down towards the water and boat pier. A screened-in porch on the back of the cottage embraces the expansive water views and provides additional space for sitting and dining.

Inside, the smaller sense of scale feels just right while still offering everything guests might need during their extended stay. It's very approachable—nothing feels overworked or superfluous. We designed the cottage interiors to be playful and casual with a melding of finishes and textures. The spacious entry with banded herringbone mosaic gray brick floors doubles as a mini mudroom with a built-in bench to change shoes or drop a handbag. A large, double cased opening with interior transom windows frames the mudroom and imparts an airiness to the space. This architectural treatment is also introduced on either side of the entry hall to create beautiful settings for artwork. To the left is the family room and to the right is the kitchen.

I love the simplicity and functionality of the kitchen. It's imbued with coastal cottage flair—open wooden shelving instead of upper cabinets and sealed wood countertops give an understated nautical look. The custom-made zinc dining table sits in the center of the room. By fabricating it at countertop height, it doubles as a kitchen island. The turn-of-the-19th-century pendants over the island impart industrial chic and historic charm.

On the other end of the hall is the cozy family room. It's full of creature comforts, with a fireplace

and a built-in wet bar with glass shelves above. David liked the juxtaposition of modern elements with more traditional ones. One unique design detail in the cottage is also one of my personal favorite touches: on the stairway leading upstairs, we fashioned the balustrade out of nautical ropes secured with stainless steel boating cleats. It's unexpected and whimsical, evoking a sailboat.

The second floor holds a larger primary suite on one end and two modestly scaled en suite bedrooms on the other. These smaller bedrooms provide just enough space to comfortably attend to a guest's needs. They are intended for a shorter stay with the idea that visitors will be mostly in the downstairs of the cottage or in other buildings on the property. This allowed us to keep the scale of guest cottage cozy and charming.

The primary suite has three major views, and we wanted to maintain glass on those three walls. We floated an interior windowed wall to create the bed backboard that allows the views to be seen when entering the room and also from the bed. What I love in this suite are the little nooks and nesting areas and the freestanding glass antique medicine cabinet in the bathroom. Every element in this building imparts a sense of historic character with whimsical turns; that's what this entire cottage is all about. It exudes a casualness that allows visitors to truly feel at home.

The guest cottage evokes an elegant yet welcoming symmetry that imparts a sense of calming order. The deep zinc-coated copper overhang conveys a casual aura and keeps the scale in check, while the curved window between the dormers nods to the main house.

PRECEDING OVERLEAF: The landscape surrounding the cottage combines manicured elements with rows of clipped boxwood and looser plantings such as grasses and hydrangeas. OPPOSITE: Clay-colored herringbone brick greets guests at the threshold, while a washed gray brick version in the foyer complements the blue front door. ABOVE: The cottage's wraparound porch offers multiple places to take in both estate and water views. Flanking the front door sit two generous blue custom benches with beadboard detailing that adds a nautical note.

OPPOSITE: The entry foyer includes both industrial and naval elements: a circular mirror gives the impression of a loop of ropes, while the simple iron lantern is in keeping with the cottage's understated charm. ABOVE: A whimsical conversation piece includes a unique stair rail fashioned from nautical ropes and stainless-steel boating cleats. The engineering was a bit tricky, but the result is a magical nod to the sailing life on the Eastern Shore. OVERLEAF: The kitchen's sealed-wood countertops, shining white subway tile, open wooden upper shelves, and blue farmhouse pendants impart a casual, come sit-down attitude.

Blue accents continue in the primary bedroom with an upholstered wood-frame chair, a pair of blue striped armchairs, and a chest of drawers. Placing the bed against a windowed interior wall embraces the views and gives the feeling of being in a tree house. OVERLEAF: The rear exterior is just as charming as the front of the cottage and includes screened-in porches for year-round enjoyment as well as a series of white Adirondack chairs behind a low fieldstone wall for sunning and embracing the shoreline.

THE ENTERTAINING BARN

When most of us think of a barn, we think of a simple rustic structure, painted red with a weather vane on top, and used for agricultural purposes. This barn is so much more. During our planning phase, the initial proposition was a large, multipurpose entertaining structure. My question was how many people we needed to seat if the structure was used for a fundraising event. The answer was 150. On a very practical note, that means you need room for fifteen ten-top tables, and it was this information that determined the scale of the barn. But of course, entertaining involves many other needs.

One question I ask all my clients who are contemplating a space like this is "How do you want to use it?"—for entertaining, living, playing, or all three? This particular structure falls mostly into the playing venue, though it works well for parties and family weddings too.

The initial inspiration for this structure came from the large barns in Pennsylvania and upstate New York. However, in the context of this estate, the barn also needed to be in harmony with its neighbors. We employed similar materials

and design references as seen throughout the compound. There's fieldstone, vertical cypress wood painted siding, and a large, open, timber-framed cupola for natural light and ventilation in the center core. This cupola greets similar smaller ones in its sight line. Select elements speak to such distinct barn-inspired style as operable board-and-batten shutters with iron hinges, six shed dormers, and sizable sliding barn doors at both the entrance from the parking court and the patio side of the building. These barn doors are always kept in the open position to expose the large glass entry doors. The barn is sited so that it balances the guest cottage across the compound's center axis. On approach, it may seem just another beautiful structure among many, but when you step inside, you have a sense of what's afoot.

Rich, sealed Douglas fir timber provides the interior framing with scissor-style trusses. We utilized black hardware strapping on the trusses to accomplish the aesthetic feel that our client envisioned. Pine decking material completes the walls, while pressure-treated decking board on the floor can stand up to vigorous sports and whatever else that you throw at it. Double-height windows and French doors on one side flood the barn with light and bring the outdoors and water views in. The support spaces are on the opposite end of the view to provide a serving/beverage area as well as two bathrooms. A staircase wraps that core utility

OPPOSITE & OVERLEAF: The entertaining barn exudes both elegance and farmhouse charm with stacked stone, sliding barn doors, large glass entry doors, shed dormers, and a cedar shake roof.

137

portion and goes down from one side to the lower-level storage and catering spaces; it rises from the other side to a small loft gaming area.

On the decorative side, the barn called for some rustic accents, such as the vintage signs that are sprinkled throughout. A cluster of bistro chairs hangs in stacks along one wall and on another is an array of identical antique galvanized and perforated metal buckets—both feel like art installations. Six custom-made iron pendant lights hang above, each five feet in diameter. Scale is especially important in a space like this, and these fixtures needed to be huge to make sense.

Because the barn needed to provide for multiple types of entertaining—from cocktail parties and seated dinners to crab feasts and children's birthday fun—the catering operations were a critical part of the design. These spaces for the barn are located on a lower level with easy access from both inside and outside. The barn nests into a falling grade, allowing a fully accessible lower level. You can drive up to and walk into this lower floor from outside straight into the catering and storage spaces. The property also allows for a perfect tent site when there's a bigger crowd, such as for a wedding.

Guests can also spill out onto a connecting outdoor terrace with a fieldstone fireplace and seating areas, water feature, and dining table. And, while the outdoor terrace increases the entertaining footprint, it also serves a very practical purpose. Behind an arbor and brick retaining wall sit all the so to speak "ugly" necessities—generators and other equipment tucked out of view.

As an entertaining barn, the space conjures up merriment and maybe a little mischief. It is a place to celebrate and toast family, friends, and colleagues. You can almost hear the champagne glasses clinking to welcome a new member of the family with an engagement announcement or to honor an accomplishment by someone in your circle. However, it also offers many other amusements and activities, such as a dance party, shuffleboard, or dodge ball. In an upstairs loft sit a ping-pong table and an office. The dimensions of a pickleball court are painted on the floor and an easy-to-move, collapsible net is at the ready. The interior barn doors close over the serving/beverage area to act as a backboard for the basketball hoop with half court markings indicated on the floor. In the grand scheme of this property, the barn beckons you to come explore and play and extends the enjoyment of the compound year-round because there's plenty of fun to be had even on the coldest, dreariest days.

Design references such as cupolas in varying scales repeat throughout the compound; a pair top the nearby carriage house. OVERLEAF: The barn faces the central green, flanked by the carriage house and garage.

OPPOSITE & ABOVE: The structure features board-and-batten shutters with iron hinges and a windowed, timber frame cupola topped with a weather vane goose in flight.
OVERLEAF: The lower level of the barn houses the catering operations and storage space.

The framing consists of sealed Douglas fir with scissor-style trusses and black hardware. RIGHT: The multi-use barn appeals to sports-minded guests with options for pickleball, basketball, tabletop shuffleboard below and ping-pong in the upstairs loft. OVERLEAF: The large, open framed cupola sits in the center of the structure, letting in additional light, while custom supersized pendants illuminate the evenings.

ABOVE & OPPOSITE: Multiple collections with a rustic, farm-inspired quality adorn the walls and make for interesting accents against the vertical pine paneling in the expansive space.

The barn includes many vintage pieces in the decor, such as this red boat. Chairs hang neatly on the wall ready for the next party. OPPOSITE: Let the sunshine in—one end of the barn features stunning stacked windows.

French doors can be thrown open into the side courtyard, where guests may take in the views or enjoy the stacked stone fireplace in cooler months. The mix of furnishings provides smaller groups the option of dining by candlelight under starry skies.

SUPPORTING STRUCTURES

Each of the outbuildings on the property of Northwest Point Farm plays a pivotal role in creating balance and function on this compound campus. The sheep shed marks the approach to the house and accents the oval-shaped sheep run. The carriage house and automobile garage flank the barn, creating a parking courtyard for party and event attendees, and the boathouse is the marker to the pier as well as a jewel box in the landscaped yard of the bocce ball court. These supporting structures serve critical roles in the daily compound functions while also delighting the eye as part of the landscape.

Every building on the compound is meticulously realized; there is no hint that some serve more utilitarian purposes. The carriage house and automobile garage form a semicircle around the entertaining barn. Each nods to the other in harmony and with distinction. OVERLEAF: A fieldstone structure topped with a weather vane, glimpsed on entering the property, looks like a small cottage with its blue shutters and door—but it's actually a sheep shed.

THE SHEEP SHED

While out on the Chester River prior to building the compound, David spotted black sheep on a neighboring property and was completely captivated. He wanted a flock of his own to impart another level of interest and beauty in the landscape of Northwest Point Farm. The breed David chose is Scottish Babydoll, and each sheep has its own name. The flock and the sheep shed are one of the first sightings when approaching the estate, a sign that you will be surrounded by nature and a bucolic atmosphere.

We centered the sheep shed directly on an axis with the main house, and it serves as an exclamation point and whimsical bookend of the entire master plan for the property. The shed radiates quaintness with its fieldstone exterior, sweet little windows with blue shutters, wood shake roof, and cupola. The three-sided structure opens on the pasture side so the sheep can find shelter from the sun; a farmhouse-style fence extends from each side to complete the enclosure. The captivating appeal of the sheep shed sets the initial tone for the entire compound.

Black sheep complete the bucolic feel of a working farm. They have names and are part of the family. OPPOSITE: The siting of the sheep shed provides a bird's-eye view to the main house. Blowsy blooms of limelight hydrangeas imbue the shed with a sense of natural charm.

THE CARRIAGE HOUSE

The carriage house's primary function is to house two utility vehicles for exploration of this expansive property. We designed it with a pair of identical doors on both sides of the structure so the vehicles can drive straight through the building. Because incoming visitors are greeted by the back side of the carriage house after driving around the sheep pasture, the rear had to be just as pretty as the front. It's dramatically symmetrical with deep gable rooflines, shed dormers, and two cupolas.

Inside, the left wing of the carriage house is a room that stores hunting gear and is intended to be used as a space for cleaning guns and loading ammunition. Maryland's Eastern Shore is well known for its vast natural resources, including white-tailed deer, ducks, and birds for seasonal hunting. The carriage house also supports a sporting clay area located in the adjacent woods. In the right wing of the structure sits a potting area that contains a large concrete countertop and sink used by the gardeners to manage dozens of potted containers on the grounds. The carriage house, a favorite of mine, presents so beautifully in the landscape, with both elegant and informal attributes that make it a pleasure to experience.

Surprises delight and offer lighthearted pauses throughout the property, including a grouping of dogs fashioned in grapevine twigs situated on the main green lawn. White picket fences provide definition and cottage casualness. OVERLEAF: The multipurpose carriage house is wrapped up in a symmetrical bearing, incorporating twin weather vane–topped cupolas, shed dormers, and dramatic gables.

THE AUTOMOBILE GARAGE

One of the first buildings we completed was the three-car garage. This was a strategic decision as it allowed the contractor to house materials during construction. The structure is sited for convenience close to the hunt room on the left side of the main house. A lovely covered breezeway guides you from the garage to the hunt room's two Dutch doors. During this walk, you begin to experience the property's relationship to the surrounding body of water.

The garage sits directly across from the carriage house; both structures are bookends to the entertaining barn, creating an engaging trio on the compound. The architecture of the garage nods to the main house with three identical gabled dormers and a white cedar shake roof. Its cupola mirrors one of the two cupolas on the carriage house opposite, creating a harmonious sight line between the buildings, while the larger cupola of the barn looks down on its more modestly scaled, but equally handsome neighbors. Lastly, sweet gable-end flower boxes mark both this structure and the carriage house, as well as the guesthouse opposite, tying all three buildings together.

The garage connects to the main house through an arbored breezeway. While it is in harmony with its neighbors, as are all the buildings on the compound, the garage offers up distinct design references, such as three narrow gables above a long, single white shingle overhang and high peaked roof. OVERLEAF: From the dewy mist of early morning to the pink skies of the sunset and twinkling evening lights, the trio of outbuildings presents a picture of orderly composition and composure.

THE BOATHOUSE

In every project we work on, we strive for that magical blend of function and beauty; you don't want to sacrifice one for the other. The boathouse reflects this principle in a thoughtful way. It's sited 100 feet from the water and aligns with the dock and boats beyond. It supports all the Chesapeake Bay water activities available on the property, including paddleboarding, fishing, kayaking, and boating. In design terms, the boathouse is basically a square with an open center core and clever function on both the exterior and interior walls.

To give it a coastal attitude, we included a pair of porthole windows on either side and a large, ventilated cupola whose slightly exaggerated scale gives the boathouse a distinction within the whole of the compound. The two exterior walls include pairs of large doors that expose the wall area for resting paddleboards, oars, and so on. The interior opens up to a wall of hooks for fishing rods and life jackets. The trellis work around the exterior looks enchanting when the climbing roses are in bloom.

ABOVE & OPPOSITE: The boathouse folly is a study in practicality and winsome charm, It cleverly hides away kayaks and boating accoutrements on either side, with an open center pass-through outfitted with hooks for fishing rods. Throughout the compound breezeways and arbors frame the buildings' sight lines. OVERLEAF: The walkway to the boathouse is set off by fieldstone walls with corner columns topped with stone obelisks. Abundant trees, grasses, and other plantings provide a lush, natural feeling.

THE POOL HOUSE AND POOL

The pool house, located adjacent to the pool's shallow sun shelf, presents as a refined, inviting, multipurpose jewel box with ingenious design concepts. It is truly a destination in and of itself. Aesthetically, the structure speaks to the main house with symmetry. It features Doric columns and a cedar shake roof; the cupola and sliding barn doors reference the property's other outbuildings. To impart a more casual and coastal feel, we used clapboard siding and solid louvered doors. Aligned on the center of the pool, the structure opens on both sides through a large, curved ceiling to expose the river in one direction and the pool water in the other.

In the center pavilion space of the pool house, the spectacular barrel-vaulted ceiling draws the eye up, and large, curved transom windows on each end provide definition. A windowed cupola creates a striking light-filled shaft in the ceiling above the dining table. We suspended two dramatic, custom iron lanterns from the ceiling and secured them with four chains for stability when the wind picks up. The interior offers friendly, low-key living and dining spaces, while supporting areas flank either side; to the right sits the kitchen-bar and to the left, the grill and pizza oven. Beyond that, a changing room, laundry room, full bathroom, and a closed-off space for mechanical operations can be entered from the covered exterior porches.

The strategy regarding how the exterior two large sliding barn doors operate on the pool house comes from a very well-planned approach, and it is a highly functional aspect of the design. The doors reflect layered access, so to speak, which offers entry into each space whether they are open or closed. On both sides of the entrance to the structure, the barn doors each have an integrated, operable built-in door so that whether the barn doors are in the open position or the closed position, the operable doors align for entry into the interior spaces. When the barn doors are closed, the operable doors provide access to the central dining area and lounge areas. When the barn doors are open, the operable doors align with two blue doors, one to the kitchen/bar and an opposite one to the laundry room.

The pool house was placed so as not to block the water views from the main house, but to be close enough to easily go back and forth between the two. It is sufficiently stocked, which makes even impromptu pool parties easy to manage. It has everything you need for seamless entertaining and plenty of fun whether for a barbecue cookout, pizza party, or dining by candlelight with starry skies as a backdrop.

The placement of any pool and how it will be viewed from the house is a key decision in the design process and one that we discuss at length with all clients. Do the homeowners want the pool

to be in direct view while inside the home, or do they prefer it to be less visible or located out of sight completely? Does the pool engage with the main floor of the residence or is it a destination space separate from the living floor? At Northwest Point Farm, because we had lifted the main house up four feet, we were able to nestle the pool into the landscape. This allows unimpeded landscape views from inside the main house. This strategy also means that in colder months, the pool cover is not in the sight line.

Everyone who visits this property appreciates the relationship between the back of the house and the pool area—it feels satisfyingly linear and organized with crisscrossing brick paths for access which join a fieldstone wall behind a row of boxwoods. We wrapped bluestone pavers around the pool court; another low fieldstone wall with a graceful curve on the water side provides additional definition in the space. A group of Adirondack chairs makes it the ideal spot for sunset viewing, and a flagpole marks the center of the pool with the American flag giving honor to all service members. The entire composition is beautifully executed into the land.

ABOVE & OVERLEAF: The pool house creates a well-thought-out destination within the compound. The pool sits below the sight lines from the main house, ensuring that nothing interferes with the water views beyond. This was achieved by raising the main house four feet within the landscape.

PAGES 182–83: Stately Doric columns impart an orderly presence in harmony with the main house, while a curved, wooden, barrel-vaulted ceiling evokes the hull of a ship. PRECEDING OVERLEAF: The pool court is nestled into the landscape, providing a level and seamless relationship to the water beyond. A grouping of Adirondack chairs behind a low, curved fieldstone wall creates an ideal viewing area. ABOVE: The pool house's self-contained design includes numerous functions—bar, kitchen, lounging, and dining. OPPOSITE: The evening glow of the pool house allows for al fresco dining and relaxing while enjoying sunset views. PAGES 188–89: The casual teak furnishings covered in performance fabrics stand up to year-round wear and tear.

THE ART STUDIO

The art studio was the ninth structure built at Northwest Point Farm and is located on the approach side of the compound. Its genesis sprung from a passion of David's. When he was younger, he learned to throw clay on a pottery wheel. The studio allows him to return to that craft, which was the original intent here. But just like the barn, the studio is a multipurpose space. Inspiration was drawn from David's grandfather's business; he owned an art gallery in Baltimore with a public gallery on the first floor and studio and work spaces on the upper floors. It was a true working studio with a large, open, well-lit space.

Originally our client's vision was an updated version of that structure, an austere brick studio with black windows. While I respected his vision, my only concern was that this aesthetic was such a departure from the estate and would not be in line with the other buildings in this harmonious, walkable compound. We wanted each building to evoke the same emotions that we had been so meticulously creating. In the end, we came up with

The art studio sits on the far right of the compound. Its abundant windows flood the interior with light, creating an airy, loft-like atmosphere. OVERLEAF: The approach to the studio deserves a pause to appreciate an enchanting fieldstone storage shed with a board-and-batten door and a peaked roof that mimics the studio aesthetic.

a beautiful compromise of stone, glass, and metal. It has become one of Kathryn's favorite buildings, and she uses it both as an office and a creative space with their daughter and others.

Upon approaching the studio, on the left, you are greeted by a modestly scaled fieldstone building with a blue beadboard door and distressed iron hardware that gives it an aged patina. This small shed is used for bike storage, but its simple elegance and details, and the way it expresses itself in the landscape, encapsulate the experience of the entire property itself in one brushstroke.

The fieldstone façade is carried through to the studio and presents a more rugged and rustic bearing as opposed to the other structures. The entrance has mahogany wooden double doors and operable, solid louvered shutters with iron detailing. These can be closed when the property is not in use. Similar shutters and doors appear upstairs as well; these design elements are a nod to the adjacent entertaining barn and connect the two buildings visually.

The interior finishes feature Douglas fir timber framing for the peaked roof, while the walls and ceiling are fieldstone and beadboard. Oversized windows on opposite sides of the studio, as well as a pyramid skylight along the upper ridge, flood the space with natural light from sunrise to sunset. The airiness of the space is palpable and truly captures the atmosphere of an artist's loft. Along one side of windows are floating shelves with iron struts that extend all the way up to the ceiling beam with distressed wooden boards—these details impart that industrial vibe

David wanted to capture.

Under the shelves, a long, white, painted built-in with iron legs, storage drawers, and an extra-long sink with four brass faucets brings fabulous functionality. Under the windows on the opposite side lives a long, low wooden bookcase. Per David's vision, we took advantage of the ceiling height in this structure and finished the upper areas as open sleeping lofts accessed by symmetrical ladders on each end. I can hear the grandchildren clamoring to stay here; there's a total feel of a sleepaway camp.

As far as the décor, the client went for the impression that a lot of the furnishings and accessories came from Grandmother's attic or were discovered in the back room of a dusty antique shop. An antique, well-worn wooden center table with iron legs divides the room and provides definition in the space. Vintage adjustable stools that surround the table evoke an architect's drafting area, and a series of copper and brass pendant lights above add patinaed character befitting the atmosphere our client wanted to create.

The sitting area has brown leather sofas that will only get better with age, and the eclectic mix of pillows imparts a Bohemian note. An old trunk with brass detailing doubles as a side table and the rustic metal coffee table feels like something from a farm. In addition to a kiln and pottery wheel, there's an easel and painting and crafting supplies.

Whether used for business meetings, art projects, or sleepovers, the studio creates a true destination experience for special moments that call forth the creative spirit of anyone who visits.

The exterior design details include a balcony with iron railing and solid, swinging louvered shutters. OPPOSITE: Mahogany double doors with upper paned glass detailing feel in harmony with the colors in the fieldstone, while a large pendant adds an industrial nod. OVERLEAF: The interior of the studio features Douglas fir timber framing for a rustic yet refined look. Given the high ceilings, sleeping lofts accessed by simple ladders were included on both sides.

A custom streamlined wood table is primed for various artistic pursuits. It can stand up to spills and will only look better with time. Vintage swivel drafting chairs add to the studio character of the space. OPPOSITE: A long sink makes cleanup a breeze, while streamlined industrial shelving set against the windows provides ample storage. OVERLEAF: The intricate peaked ceiling features Douglas fir timber framing and beadboard detailing.

ABOVE & OPPOSITE: The interior design elements complement the architecture and present a collected, laid-back attitude with generous vintage leather sofas, trunks, and wire baskets—nothing is fussy or off-putting.

THE GARDENS

Along with the architecture, David had a vision for the gardens surrounding and linking the various buildings and was an active collaborator at all times. While he wanted some formality, he also desired to pay homage to the fact that this was a working farm and wished for no garden element to be too serious or feel untouchable. The focus was on the enjoyment of outdoor living and entertaining on the Chesapeake Bay's Eastern Shore, which is affectionately known as the "land of pleasant living." We also wanted to create a beautiful, balanced rhythm between the architecture and the landscape.

The central parking court and circular lawn impart a grounded presence upon arrival and create a sense of connectedness among the outdoor spaces. Each garden beyond is harmonious with its adjacent structure while feeling cohesive within the whole. For example, next to the more informal entertaining barn, Kevin Campion, of Campion Hruby Landscape Architects, and his team included a rustic stone fireplace with a large hearth and a simple wooden pergola that provide a seamless transition from the barn to the outside terrace. The garden spaces in the rear of the main house are more formal and reflective of the house itself. Stone and brick hardscaping is laid out in a very symmetrical pattern reminiscent of the adjacent exterior and interior architecture.

While individuality was important in each garden, it was also essential that there was consistency while traversing from one structure to another. Transitions needed to feel natural and engaging; nothing jarring. This goal was achieved with the repetition of boxwoods to provide unity and definition throughout the compound. Other recurring plant materials—including limelight hydrangeas and sycamore trees—provide additional continuity, while plentiful native grasses reflect the waterside setting. It was also important that whether three or three hundred people are in the garden, the space always feels comfortable and appropriate.

Kevin and his team brought an expertise in waterside properties and were respectful of what thrives in this fragile ecosystem, which is key to the longevity of the landscape. From the walkways, pergola, and fireplace to every shrub and flower, the hardscape and softscape join hands to create an extraordinary experience everywhere you walk. Perhaps the result is more than just pleasant; I daresay it's transportive and absolutely reflective of this idyllic setting.

The covered breezeway connecting the house to the garage gives way to an abundant garden path. Russian sage, Karl Foerester feather reed grass, and little lime hydrangeas soften the edges of the home and connect it seamlessly with the land.

PAGES 210–11: Boxwoods create evergreen structure for an ever-changing perennials garden around the bocce court. Decorative pots mark the entrance, and an inviting gate opens out to the river. PAGES 212–13: Rose arbors flank the bocce court and create a new axis as seen from the guesthouse, while a grid of cherry trees supports a cross axis and accents the boat house. ABOVE: A white perennial garden connects the main house and guesthouse. Flowering crape myrtle, calamint, coneflower, and roses adorn the walkway. OPPOSITE: A dancing sheep sculpture at the end of a sycamore allée makes a playful transition from garden to farm. OVERLEAF: Early morning fog creates a moody atmosphere in the garden.

OPPOSITE: Evening entertaining at the barn terrace centers around a rustic stone fireplace. ABOVE: Twin fountains with authentic water pumps—inspired by a water feature at the original home of Bunny Mellon's daughter in Middleburg, Virginia—create audible interest for passersby and gatherings alike. OVERLEAF: Meadows have replaced lawn areas to reduce energy inputs, increase habitat diversity, and enhance a pastoral aesthetic.

Acknowledgments

First, I would like to thank each of the firm's incredible clients, who for years have welcomed us into their lives and trusted us to design their homes—their sanctuaries. It is and has been truly an honor and a joy working with each of you. You have allowed me to fulfill my greatest creative passions. In particular, I want to thank David and Kathryn Williams, who came to us with a vision for Northwest Point Farm, warmly embraced the design journey, and brought passion and thoughtfulness to our collaboration. We are eternally grateful for your trust, camaraderie, and for believing in us; we loved being involved in the complete design of this multiple structure estate.

I also want to profusely thank each member of the Purple Cherry Architects team. Without your professional dedication and talent, this dream commission could never have been fully realized at this level. I am proud of and boundlessly grateful for your energy, commitment, and hunger for creative perfection.

Next, without Mark Koski, owner of GYC Group, I would not have met these fantastic clients. I have heartfelt gratitude for the introduction and for your ongoing support of our practice, for the artistry and expertise of your team, and for your becoming a trusted and valued colleague and friend. I also want to recognize Kevin Campion of Campion Hruby Landscape Architects for his unparalleled collaboration on this, and on all our projects, and for his incredibly kind and considered foreword to this book.

To all the consulting professionals who we work with—civil engineers, structural engineers, and all others—I appreciate you so much. Your expertise is invaluable to the success of each project we are fortunate enough to work on together. I also sincerely thank each of the highly skilled tradespeople who worked on Northwest Point Farm day in and day out, harsh conditions notwithstanding, for their incomparable crafts-manship. I so appreciate each and every one of you and stand in awe of your artistry.

Putting together a book like this involves the collaboration of many talented individuals, so my deepest thanks for this effort go out to the following:

To book maven Jill Cohen and her team for believing in this book and expertly navigating us through the publishing process. To photographer Durston Saylor for his immense talent and incredible eye that so beautifully captured the magic of Northwest Point Farm. To photo stylist par excellence Helen Crowther,

whose brilliance created those special details that breathe life into each photo. To Alice Doyle, who thoughtfully helped me convey in words the unfolding of this extraordinary compound, and to graphic designer Doug Turshen for his talents in utilizing countless photographs to assemble such a captivating visual presentation. Also, to publishing pro and wordsmith Madge Baird for taking a chance on me and on this book, for her endless wisdom, and for helping see it through to the finish line, along with the rest of the team at Gibbs Smith.

And last, but never least, I want to thank my dear husband, Michael, and my three beloved children, Matthew, Jason, and Samantha for their love and support. Thank you for allowing me to grow this firm, to create beautiful work, and to follow my dreams. I appreciate you and your sacrifices more than you will ever know. You are my heart and soul; this book is dedicated to you.

First Edition
28 27 26 25 24   5 4 3 2 1

Published by
Gibbs Smith
P.O. Box 667
Layton, Utah 84041
1.800.835.4993 orders
www.gibbs-smith.com

Designed by Doug Turshen with David Huang

Library of Congress Control Number: 2023951900
ISBN: 978-1-4236-6588-5

Printed in China using FSC® Certified materials

MIX
Paper from
responsible sources
FSC® C104723